CREATION AND RECREATION

NORTHROP FRYE

Creation and Recreation

University of Toronto Press
Toronto Buffalo London

Canadian Cataloguing in Publication Data

Frye, Northrop, 1912–
    Creation and recreation

    The Larkin-Stuart lectures, delivered under the
    auspices of Trinity College, University of Toronto,
    and St. Thomas Church, Jan. 30-31 and Feb. 1, 1980.
    ISBN 0-8020-6422-1 pa.
    1. Creation – Addresses, essays, lectures.
    2. Creation (Literary, artistic, etc.) – Addresses,
    essays, lectures. 3. Semantics (Philosophy) –
    Addresses, essays, lectures. 4. Theology –
    Terminology – Addresses, essays, lectures. I. Title.

BT695.F79   231.7'65   C80-094404-6

This book has been published with the assistance of the Canada
Council and the Ontario Arts Council under their block grant
programs

Preface

THESE ARE THE LARKIN-STUART LECTURES, delivered under the auspices of Trinity College in the University of Toronto and St Thomas Church, on 30, 31 January and 1 February 1980. I am greatly obliged to Trinity College and St Thomas Church for their hospitality and for the honour of their invitation to give the lectures.

The lectures draw on earlier material of mine, some of it now out of print, and, as the opening page suggests, they are also connected with an ongoing project of greater length, a study of the narrative and imagery of the Bible and its influence on secular literature. They will doubtless be made use of for the larger book, but form a unit which can be read by itself.

NF

CREATION AND RECREATION

1

I AM A LITERARY CRITIC, mainly concerned with English literature, and I have recently developed a special interest in the way that the Bible has affected the structure and imagery of that literature. The first word to attract one's notice in both fields is the word creation. Page one of the Bible says that God created the world; page one of the critic's handbook, not yet written, tells him that what he is studying are human creations. In this book I should like to look at certain aspects of the conception or metaphor of creation, as it applies to both its divine and its human context, and, also, at what effect the extending of the same word to cover these two different areas has had on our habits of thought. I know that many questions connected with the word 'creation' are among the most hackneyed topics in both religious and secular culture, and I shall try to keep clear of what seems to me likely to have bored you already. On the other hand, I chose the topic because it is hackneyed, and is therefore easier to look at with a fresh eye. Through some closed-circuiting mechanism in the human mind, certain themes seem to get things said about them that are prescribed in advance, so that they are not really explored at all, but are simply talked out, in a way familiar to members of parliament who introduce private bills. If there are students of mine among my readers, they will often catch glimpses of charted territory, but I am not offering a rehash of lecture notes.

I want to begin with what is called 'creativity' as a feature of human life, and move from there to some of the traditional religious ideas about a divine creation. It seems to me that the whole complex of ideas and images surrounding the word 'creation' is inescapably a part of the way that we see things. We may emphasize either the divine or the human aspect of creation to the point of denying the reality of the other. For Karl Barth, God is a creator, and the first moral to be drawn from this is that man is not one: man is for Barth a creature, and his primary duty is to understand what it is to be a creature of God. For others, the notion of a creating God is a projection from the fact that man makes things, and for them a divine creator has only the reality of a shadow thrown by ourselves. But what we believe, or believe that we believe, in such matters is of very little importance compared to the fact that we go on using the conception anyway, whatever name we give it. We are free, up to a point, to shape our beliefs; what we are clearly not free to do is to alter what is really a part of our cultural genetic code. We can throw out varieties of the idea of creation at random, and these, in Darwinian fashion, will doubtless descend through whatever has the greatest survival value; but abolish the conception itself we cannot.

A year or so ago, after agreeing to help teach an undergraduate course in Shakespeare, I settled down to reread one of my favourite pieces of Shakespearean criticism, Oscar

Wilde's essay on 'The Truth of Masks.' The essay, however, was one in a collected volume of Wilde's critical essays, and I find it easy to get hooked on Wilde. His style often makes him sound dated, and yet he is consistently writing from a point of view at least half a century later than his actual time. He is one of our few genuinely prophetic writers, and, as with other prophets, everything he writes seems either to lead up to his tragic confrontation with society or reflect back on it. Partly because of this, he deliberately restricts his audience. He sets up a palisade of self-conscious and rather mechanical wit, which not merely infuriates those who have no idea what he is talking about but often puts off those who do. We may get so annoyed at his dandies waving their hands languidly at thick volumes labelled 'Plato' or 'Aristotle' that we may forget that Wilde could, and did, read Greek, and that his references to classical authors are usually quite precise. So before long I was back in the world of the essay called 'The Decay of Lying,' now widely recognized to have said a great deal of what modern theories of criticism have been annotating in more garbled language ever since.

The main thesis of this essay is that man does not live directly and nakedly in nature like the animals, but within an envelope that he has constructed out of nature, the envelope usually called culture or civilization. When Wordsworth urges his reader to leave his books, go outdoors, and let nature be his teacher, his 'nature' is a north temperate zone nature which in nineteenth-century England had become, even in the Lake District, largely a human artefact. One can see the importance, for poets and others, of the remoteness and otherness of nature: the feeling that the eighteenth century expressed in the word 'sublime' conveys to us that there is such a thing as creative alienation. The principle laid down by the Italian philosopher Vico of *verum factum*, that we understand only what we have made ourselves, needs to be refreshed sometimes by the contemplation of something we did not make and do not understand. The difficulty with Wordsworth's view is in the word 'teacher.' A nature which was not primarily a human artefact could teach man nothing except that he was not it. We are taught by our own cultural conditioning, and by that alone.

We may see already that the word 'creation' involves us in a state of mind that is closely parallel with certain types of paranoia, which may give us a clue to what Wilde means by 'lying.' Our envelope, as I have called it, the cultural insulation that separates us from nature, is rather like (to use a figure that has haunted me from childhood) the window of a lit-up railway carriage at night. Most of the time it is a mirror of our own concerns, including our concern about nature. As a mirror, it fills us with the sense that the world is something which exists primarily in reference to us: it was created for us; we are the centre of it and the whole point of its existence. But occasionally the mirror turns into a real window, through which we can see only the vision of an indifferent nature that got along for untold aeons of time without us, seems to have produced us only by accident, and, if it were conscious, could only regret having done so. This vision propels us instantly into the opposite pole of paranoia, where we seem to be victims of a huge conspiracy, finding ourselves, through no will of our own, arbitrarily assigned to a dramatic role which we have been given no script to learn, in a state of what Heidegger calls 'thrownness.'

The cultural aura, or whatever it is, that insulates us from nature consists among other things of words, and the verbal part of it is what I call a mythology, or the total structure of human creation conveyed by words, with literature at its centre. Such a mythology belongs to the mirror, not the window. It is designed to draw a circumference around human society and reflect its concerns, not to look directly at the nature outside. When man finally gets around to doing that, he has to develop the special language of science, a language which becomes increasingly mathematical in idiom. Many things have to come together in a culture before science can begin, and when it does begin it does not descend from or grow out of mythology directly. Mythological statements about nature are merely grotesque or silly if they are thought of as pre-scientific explanations of it.

Early students of mythology, it is true, liked to think of it as primitive science, because that view implied such a flattering contrast between primitive visions of nature and theirs. Thus we have Frazer defining myth as mistaken notions of natural phenomena, and Max Müller speaking of mythology as a disease of language. If he had said that language was a disease of mythology, the statement would have been just as untrue, but considerably more interesting. However, this attitude was mainly a by-product of a European ideology designed to rationalize the nineteenth-century treatment of non-European peoples. Mythology is the embryo of literature and the arts, not of science, and no form of art has anything to do with making direct statements about nature, mistaken or correct. Similarly, as science does not grow out of mythology, so it can never replace mythology. Mythology is recreated by the poets in each generation, while science goes its own way.

There is a kind of painting known as *trompe l'œil*, which endeavours to render pictorial objects so accurately that the viewer might be deceived into thinking that he was looking at the real thing. *Trompe l'œil* is a quite legitimate form of painting, but the word 'deceive' indicates the paradox in it. Returning to our figure again, when it comes to representing the outer world, no painting can compare with a window pane. This principle applies much more forcibly to literature, because there is no verbal equivalent of the window pane. Words can describe things only approximately: all they do with any real accuracy is hang together, in puns, metaphor, assonances, and the self-contained fictions of grammar and syntax.

All this is contained in Wilde's conception of the creative arts as essentially forms of 'lying,' or turning away from the external world. As long as we can keep telling one another that we see the same things 'out there,' we feel that we have a basis for what we call truth and reality. When a work of literature is based on this kind of reality, however, it often tells us only what we no longer want to know. For this reason Wilde makes fun of the careful documentary realism of Zola and others which had such a vogue in his time, of Zola settling down to give us a definitive study of the Second Empire at the moment when the Second Empire had gone hopelessly out of date. But the attack on realism is a side-issue of a far more insidious disease of writing: the morbid lust for what Matthew Arnold calls seeing life steadily and seeing it whole. Recently a collection of early reviews of mine was published, and on looking over it I was amused to see how preoccupied I had been then with two writers, Spengler and Frazer, who haunted me constantly, though I was well aware all the time I was studying them that they were rather stupid men and often slovenly scholars. But I found them, or rather their central visions, unforgettable, while there are hundreds of books by more intelligent and scrupulous people which I have forgotten having read. Some of them are people who have utterly refuted the claims of Spengler and Frazer to be taken seriously. But the thinker who was annihilated on Tuesday has to be annihilated all over again on Wednesday: the fortress of thought is a Valhalla, not an abattoir.

This is not merely my own perversity: we all find that it is not only, perhaps not even primarily, the balanced and judicious people that we turn to for insight. It is also such people as Baudelaire, Rimbaud, Hölderlin, Kierkegaard, Dostoevsky, Nietzsche, all of them liars in Wilde's sense of the word, as Wilde was himself. They were people whose lives got smashed up in various ways, but rescued fragments from the smash of an intensity that the steady-state people seldom get to hear about. Their vision is penetrating because it is partial and distorted: it is truthful because it is falsified. To the Old Testament's question: 'Where shall wisdom be found?' there is often only the New Testament's answer: 'Well, not among the wise, at any rate.'

What Wilde calls realism, the attempt to base the arts on the recognizable, to find a common ground of reality with the audience, is, he suggests, a search for some kind of emotional reassurance. I hear an echo of this whenever I listen to complaints about the difficulty or obscurity of contemporary art, complaints which often take the form 'but I think a work of art ought to communicate something.' The function of the recognizable in the arts is not aesthetic but anaesthetic. A painter of cows in a field is bound to be addressing some people who want to be reminded of cows more than they want to see pictures. The cows function as a tranquillizer, so that the more genuinely attentive part of the viewer's mind is released for pictorial experience. A painter may, however, get fed up with the compromise involved, as most painters today in fact have done, and say: to hell with the cows; look at the form and colour of the picture. If this is his attitude he is not withdrawing from 'reality': he is seeing more intensely by means of his medium. The recognizable as such is, in human terms, the non-creative; it is the disturbing insight into it that we associate with the word creation.

All this has become a commonplace in a time like ours when we are so much more heavily insulated against 'nature' than we were even in Wilde's time. A glance out of the window of an aeroplane, to the patterns of the landscape or city lights below, will tell us why this is the century of Kandinsky and not that of Constable or Ruysdael; more important, it will also tell us that space for us has become a set of co-ordinated points: we do not live in a centred space any more, but have to create our own centres. In 'The Decay of Lying' Wilde is, verbally, defending the romantic against the realistic, but these are only the terms of his age: the positive thing he is defending is not the romantic but the unmediated. His point is that what is called realism is not founded on nature or reality at all. We never see these things directly; we see them only through a prism of conventionalized commonplaces, outworn formulas within the art itself, the fossilized forms of earlier attempts to escape from nature and reality. Only a distorted imagination that breaks away from all this and sees reality as a strange, wonderful, terrible, fantastic world is creative in the human sense of the term.

We are now perhaps beginning to glimpse something of the complexity of the situation we are trying to look at in this book. Traditionally, everything we associate with nature, reality, settled order, the way things are, the data of existence that we have to accept, is supposed to go back to *the* creation, the original divine act of making the world. Now we find that if we apply the word creative to human activities, the humanly creative is whatever profoundly disturbs our sense of 'the' creation, a reversing or neutralizing of it. The encounter of God and man in creation seems to be rather like what some of the great poets of nuclear physics have described as the encounter of matter with anti-matter: each annihilates the other. What seems one of the few admirable forms of human achievement, the creation of the arts, turns out to be a kind of decreation: I might have called my lectures 'Creation and Decreation' if I had not been afraid of irritating you beyond the limits even of your tolerance.

I turn the pages of my Wilde book to the next essay, 'The Critic as Artist,' and there I read near the beginning the wonderful passage about music:

After playing Chopin, I feel as if I had been weeping over sins that I had never committed, and mourning over tragedies that were not my own. Music always seems to me to produce that effect. It creates for one a past of which one has been ignorant, and fills one with a sense of sorrows that have been hidden from one's tears. I can fancy a man who had led a perfectly commonplace life, hearing by chance some curious piece of music, and suddenly discovering that his soul, without his being conscious of it, had passed through terrible experiences, and known fearful joys, or wild romantic loves, or great renunciations.

First, of course, we cannot restrict the scope of this passage to music; it applies to all the arts, though it may well be true that music has some special mystery about its evocations.

Second, we see that Wilde is postulating two levels of experience, in which one level is remembered and the other repressed, though he gives repression a very different context from Freud. Our sense experience, our memories, our established habits and rituals, all act as filters: they screen out or accommodate whatever in our lives is disturbing or threatening. 'Had we the first intimation of the Definition of Life,' said Emily Dickinson, 'the calmest of us would be Lunatics!' It is only the arts that allow this screened-out emotion and experience to return in some bearable form, and make us realize that while we have been living our lives as 'normally' as we can, we have also been, all the time, citizens of the lunatic country of Don Quixote and Captain Ahab and King Lear. That is why their moods and behaviour can be intelligible to us.

This principle of the arts evoking the real and repressed past is familiar to us from Proust, whose narrator Marcel perceives the pattern of his own real past through an accidental glimpse of it, so that he comes to the beginning of the imaginative vision of his life at the moment when his reader comes to the end of it. The implication is that what Marcel sees at the end of his experience is the possibility of looking at it in the way that the reader should have been looking at it all along. This opens up the issue of the creative reader and his role in literature, which is Wilde's main concern in this essay, and to which I shall return in the last chapter.

If we apply this principle to social and historical existence we get some simpler and more familiar data. Out of the general welter of human life, the great works of literature and music and the plastic arts have been born. There is no cultural development in the past which did not have in its background all the cruelty and folly of which mankind is capable; yet the works of culture themselves seem to be in a perpetual state of innocence. This is still true when the cruelty and folly are directly reflected from the art itself. The pottery and textiles and metalwork that we see in museums, when compared to the conditions of life that produced them, seem to float up from those conditions as, in Apuleius' story of *The Golden Ass*, the lovely fairy-tale of Cupid and Psyche floats up like a soap bubble out of the sickening brutality of its context. But, of course, we have to take the whole book, brutality and all, as a cultural product of its time, and similarly we cannot abstract some of the works of man from others. It is a gross error in perspective either to detach the cultural from the historical past or to confuse the two.

Our cultural heritage, then, is our real and repressed social past, not the past of historical record but the great dreams of the arts, which keep recurring to haunt us with a sense of how little we know of the real dimensions of our own experience. As I have insisted so often in different contexts, such words as 'classic' or 'masterpiece' mean very little except that some recurring dreams from the past refuse to go away, and remain staring at us silently until we confront them. They are the reality behind all ancestor worship, and the part of our own identity that extends into the past. It has been said that those who do not learn history are condemned to repeat it: this means very little, because we are all in the position of voters in a Canadian election, condemned to repeat history anyway whether we learn it or not. But those who refuse to confront their own real past, in whatever form, are condemning themselves to die without having been born.

The contemplation of the ordinary historical past, however, suggests another kind of vision that seems to start with us and be independent of the arts. This is the vision of what humanity might conceivably do, and what human life could conceivably be, a vision that breaks with everything man has done and is projected on the future. This social vision of a future discontinuous with history as we have known it, turning history, in Joyce's phrase, into a nightmare from which we are trying to awake, is really a vision of human redemption, though the redemptive power is not necessarily one outside ourselves. Mary Shelley records with some wonder, in her note on *Prometheus Unbound*, that 'Shelley believed that mankind had only to will that there should be no evil, and there would be none.' But surely this is the kind of reflection that must occur to everybody at some time or other. It is particularly in youth, I suppose, that one feels most strongly the absurdity of ordinary human actions, and, even more, the absurdity or wickedness of believing that they are made necessary by fate or reason or nature or the will of God. Here again, in a different context, is the sense of the crucial importance of setting free something normally repressed in ordinary human experience. And here again is a sphere of creation, though social in reference rather than individual, linked to the future rather than the past, and with the imaginary rather than the imaginative.

Sometimes this feeling clashes with the claims of the past, however impressive. Black students reading a white man's literature, women bored by heroines presented as models of virtue because they conform to male codes, radicals of all persuasions, often develop an anti-cultural streak that wants to scrap the past, including its greatest imaginative achievements, in order to start doing something else and something better. A friend of mine travelling in China during the cultural revolution wanted to see some ancient frescoes in

Peking: her guide took her there, but said impatiently that if she had her way she would cover them all up with posters explaining how exploited the people of that day were. The difference between the actual and the cultural past was of little importance for this guide compared to the urgency of changing the direction of life entirely.

It is true that our course of action in life is guided, to an extent we seldom realize, by some underlying vision of what society could be. Such a vision has to be projected on the future, but it exists only in a metaphorical future. We do not know the future at all except by analogy with the past, and the future that will happen will not be much like anyone's vision of it. This gives our social ideals the intensity and purity of something that does not exist, yet they are born out of analogy with what has come to us through tradition. So all visions of a social future must be rooted in the past, socially conditioned and historically placed. I note a comment in Jacques Lacan, in an essay discussing the role of language in psychoanalytic treatment: 'the effect of a full word is to reorder the past contingent events by conferring on them the sense of necessities to come.'

Some reactionaries deliberately model their visions of the future on a return to the past, or what they imagine to have been the past; radicals, as we generally understand the word, have a vision of the future which is more of a break with the past. But all changes of direction in society, progressive, revolutionary, reactionary, or whatever, come to a point at which they have to establish continuity with what has gone before. Some rationalizing historical construct usually appears at that point, showing how certain tactical changes in the prospective future are outgrowths of certain trends in the past. But if we are dealing with the fundamental social vision which underlies all creative action, the only element in the past deep enough to call to that deep is the tradition of human creative achievement. It is on that level of social insight that we realize why the vision of a new social order cannot be disconnected from the forms of past creation in the arts.

Wilde attempted to deal with this aspect of creation too, in his essay 'The Soul of Man under Socialism.' He remarks there that 'a map of the world that does not include Utopia is not worth even glancing at, for it leaves out the one country at which Humanity is always landing.' By 'socialism,' however, Wilde means apparently only distributing wealth and opportunity more evenly, so that all people can become pure individualists, and hence, to some degree, artists. He says that in his ideal world the state is to produce the useful, and the individual or artist the beautiful. But beauty, like nature and reality, is merely another of those reassuring words indicating a good deal of ready-made social acceptance. Wilde is preoccupied in this essay by his contempt for censorship, and is optimistic that what he calls socialism would bring about the end of the tyranny of an ignorant and mischievous public opinion. This has not been our experience of socialism or any other system since Wilde's time, and his prophetic vision in this essay seems to have gone out of focus. But, as usual, his sense of context is very accurate: he identifies the two aspects of our subject, the creation of a future society and the continuing of the creativity of the past in spite of the past. As he says: 'the past is what man should not have been; the present is what man ought not to be; the future is what artists are.'

The issue of censorship, and other aspects of social resistance to creation, is a very important one, if we are right in regarding the creative as expressing what ordinary experience represses. You will perhaps not be surprised to learn that I have no use for the lame-brained hysterics who go around snatching books by Margaret Laurence and Alice Munro out of school libraries. I also resent the mindless cliché that the best way to sell a book is to ban it, which means that all its extra readers will be attracted to it for silly reasons. But I sometimes wonder whether the work of creation in society is really effective if it meets with no social resistance at all. The conventions of painting, for example, have become so tolerated that it is difficult even to imagine what kind of pictures today would go into the *salon des refusés* to which the impressionists were exiled a century or so ago. One applauds the tolerance, except that the public is so seldom tolerant about anything unless it has become indifferent to it as well. A world where the arts are totally tolerated might easily become a world in which they were merely decorative, and evoked no sense of challenge to repression at all.

What we see continually in the world around us is a constant and steady perversion of the vision of a free and equal social future, as country after country makes a bid for freedom and accepts instead a tyranny far worse than the one it endured before. There seems no escaping the inference that the real desire for freedom and equality is not only repressed too, but is in fact one of the most deeply repressed feelings we have. And if the vision of a social future is connected with the vision of the creativity of the past, which is our main thesis here, then there must be different layers of repression appealed to by art, some much deeper than others. At the deepest layer, if we are right, the enjoyment of the arts would be as strongly resisted as any other effort at freedom.

Human life consists of leisure and work, and these provide the bases for, respectively, our visions of past art and social future. To the extent that leisure and work have been represented by different classes of society, each has been fostered on a rather superficial level. The leisure class on top was supposed to enjoy the world of culture as a special privilege; the working class below was supposed to work without a vision of any social future of which they could form a part. It seems to me that this set-up is slowly rearranging itself: the phrase 'leisure class' no longer means very much anywhere now, and the phrase 'working class' would probably not mean very much either if it had not become a pious cliché. Work and leisure are gradually becoming different aspects of the same life, not two different classes in society. But the old class habits keep persisting, at least in our thinking. It has puzzled many people that it is possible for someone, the commandant of a Nazi death camp, for example, to have a cultivated taste for the arts and still be what he is. It is possible because the response to the arts can also exist on an aesthetic level, of the sort indicated by Wilde's term 'beautiful,' where they are objects to be admired or valued or possessed.

But the arts actually represent an immense imaginative and transforming force in society, which is largely untapped because so much of our approach to them is still possessive and aesthetic. There is a much deeper level on which the arts form part of our heritage of freedom, and where inner repression by the individual and external repression in society make themselves constantly felt. That is why totalitarian societies, for example, find themselves unable either to tolerate the arts or to generate new forms of them. During the Nazi occupation of France, the French discovered that one of the most effective things they could do was to put on classical plays like *Antigone* or *The Trojan Women*, in original or adapted versions. The Nazis had no excuse for censoring them, but because of the intense repression all around, the plays began to mean something of what they really do mean.

As for the life of work, the more alienating and less creative it becomes, the more completely it becomes an observance of time, a clock-punching and clock-watching servitude. Leisure begins in the breaking of the panic of time, that unhurried commitment in which alone the study of the arts, which take their own speeds, is possible. On the aesthetic or possessive level there is still a preoccupation with time. We read at the end of Walter Pater's *Renaissance*:

We are all under sentence of death, but with a sort of indefinite reprieve ... we have an interval, and then our place knows us no more. Some spend this interval in listlessness, some in high passions, the wisest, at least among 'the children of this world,' in art and song. For our one chance lies in expanding that interval, in getting as many pulsations as possible into the given time.

The panic of the phrase 'as many as possible' indicates that for Pater the pursuit of experience has not yet broken free of the tyranny of time, nor of the aesthetic level of response which is really a collecting of impressions. In contrast, we have Marcel Duchamp, the painter of the 'Nude Descending the Staircase,' speaking of a picture as a 'delay':

Use 'delay' instead of 'picture' or 'painting'; 'picture on glass' becomes 'delay in glass' ... It's merely a way of succeeding in no longer thinking that the thing in question is a picture – to make a 'delay' of it in the most general way possible ...

This conception has been considerably expanded in our day by Jacques Derrida and others, where distancing in both time and space becomes central to the contact of text and reader.

To the extent that work becomes creative, it tends to incorporate and be based on a vision of an ideal society projected on the future. If we turn to biblical imagery, we can see that the core of this vision is that of the humanized creation out of nature that I spoke of at the beginning. So far, in speaking of creation in the Bible, I have referred only to the somewhat confusing activities of God at the beginning, who creates the world in Genesis 1, creates paradise in Genesis 2, destroys paradise in Genesis 3, and destroys the rest of the world in the deluge of Genesis 6. As a creator, the deity seems to have had other things on his infinite mind, or perhaps, as a poem of Thomas Hardy suggests, he had no real talent for creation at all. But there is also a partly human vision of creation in the Bible, associated with a future restoration of Israel to its Promised Land. Man lives, we said, isolated from nature by his own culture, and this culture is partly a technical achievement and partly a visionary one. At the centre of the technical achievement is his transformation of a part of his natural environment into a nature with a human shape and a human meaning. In biblical imagery we begin with the fruit trees and fresh water of paradise, and then go through various phases of social development: the pastoral phase of flocks and herds, the agricultural phase of harvest and vintage, and the urban phase of cities, buildings, streets, and highways.

Similar imagery lies at the heart of every mythology and every development of the arts, and indicates that what man really wants is what his genuine work shows that he wants.

When he is doing genuine work, that is, not making war or feeding a parasitic class, he is making a human artefact out of nature. Whatever the status of 'the' creation ascribed to God at the beginning, there is another creation which involves human effort, and the idealized forms of this creation are again projected on the future. I call this 'recreation,' or the counter-movement of creation set up by man. The destructive activities assigned to God in Genesis provide the motivation for this, and his original creative activities, such as the planting of the garden of Eden, provide the models.

But while all cultures reflect similar patterns of imagery in regard to nature, the Bible is distinctive in its attitude to nature. I shall be looking at this in more detail tomorrow night, but the general principle is that for the Bible there is nothing numinous, no holy or divine presence, within nature itself. Nature is a fellow creature of man: to discover divine presences in nature is superstition, and to worship them is idolatry. Man, according to the Bible, has to look to himself, his institutions, and more particularly his records of verbal revelation, to find the structural principles of the creation he is entrusted with.

Further, and by the same principle, the solution of the major human and social problems have to precede the real recreation of nature. We are gradually beginning to realize that the exploitation of man by man is evil, and not merely evil but unnecessary. Human nature being what it is, the transforming of some of the natural environment into a humanized one has not been wholly a creative operation: there has been an immense amount of spoiling, wasting, destroying, and plundering as well. But only recently have we come to feel much uneasiness of conscience about this: our cultural traditions insist that nature was provided for the sake of man, and that the unlimited and uninhibited exploitation of nature has nothing to be said against it, except that we obviously have to call a halt after we have used up everything there is.

This view of nature as an unlimited field of exploitation is found in most human cultures, but with us is peculiarly a legacy of our biblical and Christian inheritance. We notice that the prophets in the Bible, when they speak of a final restoration of Israel, also speak of a regenerating of nature and a reconciliation with it, but they emphasize that this can take place only after man has stopped the destructive activities within himself. Hosea says, for instance:

And in that day will I make a covenant for them with the beasts of the field, and with the fowls of heaven, and with the creeping things of the ground: and I will break the bow and the sword and the battle out of the earth, and will make them to lie down safely.

The implication is that the regenerating of human society must precede, though it forms a part of, the regeneration of nature.

The Bible has little or nothing to say about man's cultural past, and to that extent is deficient as a guide to human creative perspectives. The traditions of the literary critic are of classical origin, and for this aspect of our subject we have to depend mainly on secular literature. I began by referring to a course on Shakespeare that I had recently agreed to help teach, and in looking over the texts of Shakespeare I found myself once again absorbed, as I have been all my critical life, by the immense profundity and complexity of social vision in the final romances, *Pericles*, *Cymbeline*, *The Winter's Tale*,

The Tempest. I noticed, as I had noticed before, that they resemble the earlier comedies, but differ from them in that they seem to contain a tragic action as well as a comic one, instead of merely avoiding a tragic conflict as the earlier comedies do. I had realized for a long time that the comic vision in literature is one which is very close to what I have been calling the vision of a future society. In comedy a certain drive to freedom, generally symbolized by the impulse of two young people to marry, is being thwarted by something foolish and obstinate in the social order which nevertheless has control of that order temporarily. But normally, at the end of a comedy, the drive towards freedom succeeds, its opponents or blocking figures are baffled, and the action ends with most of the characters together on the stage, suggesting a new society being formed at the end of the play. The ideals of this new society have to be left undefined, because its activities are assumed to begin after the play itself is over.

Sometimes, more particularly in *The Winter's Tale*, this comic action is associated or identified with the fertility imagery of a renewal of nature, as spring succeeds winter and new life emerges from old. In *The Winter's Tale* the great sheep-shearing festival scene in the fourth act depicts the determination of two young people, Florizel and Perdita, to marry in the teeth of parental opposition, and in the background is the triumphant renewing vitality of 'great creating nature,' as spring in Bohemia follows hard on winter in Sicilia. But at the same time that Shakespeare gives us this vision of youth and spring victorious over age and winter, he puts as much or even more emphasis on the reintegrating of an older generation. It is the reunion of Leontes and Hermione, where the past folly and obsession of Leontes is cast out, that forms the final scene, and this scene is as closely associated with art as that of Florizel and Perdita is with nature. It takes place in a chapel, an alleged work of painting and sculpture comes to life, and the miracle is accomplished by music and poetry. It seems as though two things must happen if either is to happen: there is a vision of a happy social future, but there is also a vision of a reintegrated past in which dead things come to life again under the spell of art.

All the romances seem to have something of this double resolution, of young people forming the nucleus of a new social order and a new outburst of fertility, and of older people restored to their original lives through the arts, the arts often being represented simply by music. In *The Tempest* the young lovers, Ferdinand and Miranda, are shown by Prospero the masque which symbolizes their future lives, where the main characters are Ceres, Juno, and Iris, the earth, the sky, and the rainbow, deities of fertility and promise. They are then ready to encounter what Miranda calls a brave new world. At the same time Prospero, whose art is symbolized by magic, though it consists very largely of music and drama, is reintegrating his own past as Duke of Milan, transforming the society of his former enemies into a new shape.

In this play the reintegrating of the past through art and the renewal of the future through the energy of youth and nature are contrasted with the mere past and the mere future. The mere past, where everything vanishes into darkness and annihilation, is evoked by Prospero's great 'end of the revels' speech; the mere future is what we see in Prospero's return to Milan, to be as absent-minded and ineffectual a Duke as he was before. The positive action of the play, therefore, where reintegration and renewal both take place, is not in the past or future at all, but in an expanded present where, as Eliot says, the past and the future are gathered.

This present is a resurrection which is not the reviving of a corpse, and a rebirth which is not an emerging of a new life from a dying older body to die in its turn. It is rather a transfiguration into a world we keep making even when we deny it, as though a coral insect were suddenly endowed with enough consciousness and vision to be able to see the island it has been helping to create.

2

I N THE PREVIOUS CHAPTER I spoke of human life as contained within a cultural envelope that insulates it from
nature, and said that the verbal part of this envelope is, or at
least starts out as, a mythology. A mythology is made up of
myths, and so I should first of all try to explain what the
word myth means in the sense, or senses, in which I shall be
using it. As a literary critic, I want to anchor the word myth
in its critical context. Myth to me, then, means first of all
mythos or narrative, words arranged in a sequential order.
Every structure in words designed for sequential reading,
which excludes practically no structures except telephone
books, has a narrative, a *mythos*, a sequential ordering that
begins, in our culture, on the top left-hand corner of page
one and ends at the bottom right-hand corner of the last
page. Naturally there is a great variety of myths or narratives: some are stories, some arguments, some descriptions,
and so on.

However, the use of the term in so broad and general a
sense would entangle us in a discussion of the different
shapes that language and thought assume, which enable a

myth in some contexts to take the form of an argument or a description. We have no time for that, so I shall restrict the word myth to its more familiar sense of culturally early narratives, which come from a time when concepts and arguments and abstractions had not yet appeared in language. Such myths are stories, or sequential acts of personified beings. Every culture produces a mythology of this concrete kind, and it is out of the story patterns contained in such a mythology that literature develops.

My own interest in myth begins with its literary development: to me a literary myth is not a contaminated myth but a matured one. In my perspective as a literary critic the 'real meaning' of a myth emerges slowly from a prolonged literary life, and then its meaning includes everything it has effectively been made to mean during that life. What the Song of Songs 'really means,' for example, is not confined to the village wedding songs and late echoes of fertility ritual out of which it may have originated, but includes what it has been made to mean in Bernard of Clairvaux and St John of the Cross, where it expresses the love of Christ for his people. Theoretically, there is no analogy between a myth and a species: a poet can do what he likes with his myth, and can marry it to any other myth and still produce imaginative offspring. But what is theoretically possible and what poets actually do seem to be different: in practice, poets show a great respect for the integrity of the myths they treat. Samuel Butler remarked that a chicken was merely an egg's device for producing more eggs; similarly, a poet often seems to be merely a myth's device for reproducing itself again in a later period.

Anthropologists, on the other hand, and others who are interested primarily in the immediate social and cultural functions of myths, find myths most useful to them at the earliest possible stage, before the free play of the creative imagination has begun to turn them into what we think of as literature. The distinction between myth and literature is strictly speaking impossible, as no myth can exist except in some sort of narrative formulation, but still it is possible to isolate, in some cultures, what is essentially a pre-literary mythology. In the highly developed cultures surrounding the Bible the problem hardly exists. Myth and literature are already indistinguishable in the Gilgamesh epic, which is much older than any part of the Bible.

But the Bible is exceptional in having a strongly doctrinal emphasis, in its story of creation, which is clearly not intended to be primarily literary or imaginative. What it is intended to be will, I hope, become clearer as we go on, but we have to approach it first on the poetic level all the same. The status of the opening of Genesis as a factual historical record is no longer an issue for many of us, and to try to accept it as one is merely running scared. To go back to the argument of Oscar Wilde's essay on 'The Decay of Lying' discussed in the previous chapter, it is only when the creation story is considered factually false that it can be of any conceivable use to us. The hero of Eliot's *Family Reunion* complains that his family understands 'only events, not what has happened.' It is myth, and only myth, that tells us what has happened.

It becomes clear in many modern studies of myth, such as those of Mircea Eliade, that it is only when a myth is accepted as an imaginative story that it is really believed in. As a story, a myth becomes a *model* of human experience, and its relation to that experience becomes a confronting and present experience. The truth of the story of the fall of Adam and Eve does not depend on the possibility that an archaeologist may eventually dig up their skeletons. It depends on its power to convey the present sense of alienation in human consciousness, the sense of being surrounded by a nature not ours. Such a myth bears the same relation to the law in the first five books of the Bible that a parable of Jesus bears to the teaching of the gospel.

Milton's *Paradise Lost* is a poem about the creation of the world and the fall of man written by a poet convinced of the factual reliability of the Biblical story. Yet even Milton draws a distinction between the kind of instruction that the unfallen Adam receives from Raphael and the instruction that the fallen Adam receives from Michael. Raphael tells Adam the story of the fall of Satan, which except for an allusion or two in the Bible is entirely Milton's invention. The implication is that teaching by means of parables is the only appropriate kind of teaching for a free man. Michael summarizes for Adam the story of the Bible, events which are future to Adam but will certainly occur, implying that man's freedom of will has been curtailed to the vanishing point. All Milton's reverence for the Bible as a book of promise and a charter of human freedom cannot conceal the fact that this kind of knowledge is debased and sinister knowledge: that is, knowledge of an already determined future is part of the forbidden knowledge that Adam should never have had.

Our next task is to bring out the peculiar characteristics of the story of creation in Genesis as a myth. The word mythology implies, by its very existence, that story-myths have a tendency to stick together to form an interconnected series of stories. It would be usual for such a mythology to begin with a creation myth, and there are as many varieties of creation myths as there are societies to produce them. In the early

Near Eastern and Mediterranean cultures that we are concerned with, however, two types of creation myth seem to dominate. Perhaps it will be easiest to explain this by a creation myth of my own about creation myths. Let us assume a primeval myth-maker, standing alone in the garden of Eden, about to design a creation myth *a priori*, wholly detached from his social context and conditioning. No such person could exist, but we may learn something from postulating him. The kind of creation myth he will come up with, then, will depend on whether he is looking up or down at the time he is constructing it.

If he looks down, he sees the earth with its progression of seasons, the place from which all living things, animals and plants, are born and to which they return when they die. A creation myth based on these phenomena would be a sexual creation myth, assuming that the world took shape originally in the same way that it still renews itself every spring, or renews life in birth. In the beginning there was winter, and then came the spring; or, in the beginning there was a female body, and something got born from it. No feature is invariable or without many exceptions in mythology, but one very obvious figure for such a myth to focus on would be that of an earth-mother, the womb and tomb of all life. For such an earth-mother, from whom all living things emerge and to whom all dying things return, would be the direction of all death as well as the source of all life, and would consequently have a sinister aspect as well as a cherishing one. The cycle over which she would preside is what Plato might call the cycle of the different. Newborn animals are not the reborn forms of their parents; the flowers that bloom in the spring are not the same as those that bloomed last spring.

One immensely simplifying principle in such a creation myth is that death, along with the pain and solitude that go with it, would not be a problem. Death is built in to a myth which is primarily a myth about living things, all of which die. Life is unintelligible without death: there may be a continuous force that propels the birth of new life, but such a life-force merely uses the individual: it does not exist for his sake.

If our myth-maker looks up, he sees the cycle of the sun and the slower cycle of the moon. This suggests rather a cycle of the same: it seems to be unmistakably the same sun that comes up the next morning, the same moon that waxes and wanes, and in the background, except for the five planets that also have their appointed courses, there are, as it seems, the cycling but unchanging stars. We hear of some societies that 'believe' that a new sun is created each day: anthropologists in particular are fond of reminding us that some societies will believe anything, including no doubt some societies of anthropologists. However, our assumed myth-maker is not believing anything yet: he is merely constructing. Milton, speaking of pagan mythology, uses the phrase 'they fabled,' instead of 'they believed': it sounds more tendentious, and Milton meant it to be so, but it is also more accurate, because fabling, unlike belief, is an activity that we can get some evidence for. For this version of creation mythology, the periodic return of the sun, moon, and stars sets the pattern for the cycle of the seasons, reflecting the work of an intelligent being who, like the God of the Old Testament, does not change, or, like the creating deity of Plato's *Timaeus*, imitates such a being.

The sky-begotten creation myth, then, would suggest the subordinating of becoming to being, of cyclical change to a power of stability that controls cyclical change and is not subject to it. Such a creation myth would not start with birth from sexual union but with some power assumed to be superior to both. It would be, in short, an artificial creation myth. The world must originally have been made, including the world of living things, however universal the process of birth and death may still be among living things. And just as the sexual creation myth most readily suggests an earth-mother, so the artificial myth would correspondingly suggest a sky-father. Sky, because of the predominance of the heavenly bodies in the materials of the myth, and father, because this creator goes about his own mysterious business without nursing his children.

An artificial creation myth suggests planning and intelligence, and planning and intelligence suggest a creator who could have originally produced only a perfect or model world, a world with no death or disease or decay in it at all. This model world is apparently the one described as being made in the first chapter of Genesis, where every aspect of creation calls for the comment 'and God saw that it was very good,' so good that he spent the seventh day of creation contemplating it. To account for the contrast between the model world that such a God must have made and the actual world that we find ourselves in now, a myth of a human 'fall' must be added, an alienation myth which expresses the present human condition but does not attach it directly to the work of creation. Even in Plato's *Timaeus*, just mentioned, where the world is made by a demiurge, an artificer working in imitation of a model, whatever is wrong with our world is presumably part of the great failure of all imitations to reproduce their models accurately that, for Plato, recurs in human art.

The question 'when did it all begin?', however inevitable it may seem, is a totally unanswerable question, because it is impossible to conceive a beginning of time. One may of course say that there was a creation which created time as well as everything else, or that our perception and experience of time are a result of our fallen state, but these are only verbal formulas concealing the fact that the beginning of time is an unthinkable thought. The sexual creation myth is no better off: to the problem of whether the chicken or the egg came first there is no answer. St Augustine mentions someone who, irritated by questions about what God was doing 'before' he made the world, said he was preparing a hell for those who ask such questions. This is really another way of saying that the doctrine of divine creation is among other things a linguistic device for shutting off the question 'what happened before anything else happened'? There is nevertheless an essential imaginative issue bound up with the word 'beginning,' which is the opening word of the Bible. We derive our notions of beginnings and ends from our own births and deaths, the two crucial events in which we first join a moving belt of phenomena and finally drop off it. The moving belt itself cannot really be thought of as beginning or ending, but, because *we* begin and end, we insist that beginning and ending must be somehow much more important than merely continuing.

Hence the artificial creation myth, where the world was made by an intelligent sky-father, the one that wins out in the biblical tradition, is also a myth in which an absolute beginning is postulated, as something superior to all the continuity which follows. In the complete form of the myth an absolute beginning implies an absolute end. But such an end would have to be the end of death, not of life, a death of death in which life has become assimilated to the unending. Thus the biblical creation myth takes us back to one of the most 'primitive' of all views: that death, the most natural of all events, the one thing we know will always happen, is nevertheless somehow wrong and unnatural, not part of the original scheme of things. The author of the Book of Wisdom gazes serenely at the facts of his experience, every one of which confirms the law that there are no exceptions to dying, and remarks: 'For God made not death; the generations of the world are healthful; and there is no poison of destruction in them, nor is there a kingdom of death upon the earth.'

The sense of the importance of beginning and ending in traditional Christianity has in it a thick streak of what last night we called paranoia, and has produced some very bizarre situations. In the seventeenth century, the age of Galileo and Newton, biblical scholars were still gravely explaining that the time of creation was probably the spring equinox of 4004 BC, around two in the afternoon. And during the past century there have been several assemblages of faithful gathered to await an 'end of the world,' often on the top of a mountain, the existence of which in itself indicates many millions of years of both age and of life expectancy for the earth.

For the artificial or sky-father myth, the metaphorical kernel for this conception of a total 'beginning' would not be birth, but the experience of waking up from sleep. It is in the process of awakening to consciousness that we are most clearly aware of the sense of a beginning in a world both new and familiar, which we are quite sure is real, whatever the world 'before' it was. The curious insistence in the biblical account on a sequence of 'days,' and the recurring refrain 'and the evening and the morning were the first day,' etc., seem to be emphasizing the importance of this metaphor. In Milton's *Paradise Lost* and Michelangelo's Sistine Chapel the sense of the creation of Adam as an awakening of consciousness out of the sleep of matter is even stronger.

How there could be uncomplicated 'days' of creation when the sun was created only on the fourth day is an old puzzle, and even St Augustine felt that if God said 'days' he must have had some mental reservation about the word. Yet the institution of the Sabbath, and the importance given to the calendar week, seem still to be based on the connection of creation with the contrast of day and night, waking and sleeping. The fact that even in contemporary English the words 'sunlight' and 'daylight' are different words may suggest a remote period in which daylight was not causally associated with the sun, but it is doubtful if the original 'light' of Genesis can be reduced to this kind of confusion.

It is natural to think that the earth-mother myth is the older of the two, being the myth more appropriate for an agricultural society, as its rival was for the more urban, tool-using, and patriarchal society that succeeded it. Certainly in Hesiod, one of the fountain-heads of Greek mythology, the sky-father Zeus is thought of as a relative late-comer, the third at least of a series of sky-gods, who establishes his supremacy by force over a much older earth-mother. The latter retires sullenly below with her defeated titans, chthonic powers who, either as titans or as giants, meet us many times in many mythological guises. In the first chapter of Genesis the artificial sky-father myth seems to have it all his own way. But there are two creation myths in Genesis, and the second or so-called Jahwist one, which begins in Genesis 2:4, is clearly much the older. In this account we start with the watering of a garden. The garden is a symbol of the female body in the Bible, recurring in the Song of Songs, where the body of the bride is described as 'a garden enclosed, a fountain sealed.' In the same account, too, Adam is formed (Genesis 2:7) from a feminine *adamah* or dust of the ground. Not all the sexual myth has been excluded: enough has been vestigially left in to suggest that some still earlier creation myths are being incorporated.

However, both creation myths in the Bible seem at first sight intolerably patriarchal. Deity is associated exclusively with the male sex; man was created first and woman out of his body, in contrast to the later 'fallen' cycle of birth from a mother; the fall was precipitated by the female, and as a result the male is to have dominance over her. There is no question that the story has got mixed up with patriarchal social ideology, and no question either that it has been constantly invoked and ruthlessly exploited to rationalize doctrines of male supremacy. But within the myth itself, there is an element in the symbolism of male and female which is distinguishable from the social relations of men and women. It would be useful if Western thought had developed something like the classical Chinese conceptions of *yang* and *yin*, which would express something of the imaginative and mythological relations of male and female without perverting them in this way. Aristotle, for example, remarked that sex was an analogue to his distinction of form and matter, without drawing morals about the social superiority of males. But there is probably no such thing as an unperverted myth, nor is there likely to be for a long time.

The myth of a fall, being as we said an alienation myth, expresses the sense that the identity we are given at birth is, somehow or other, not our real or our whole identity. Such a sense is readily connected with the conception of God as a parent, because the parent stands for the whole of whatever has existed before us that has made our own existence possible. As that, the parent is the handiest symbol to express the feeling that we are born with an unknown identity which is both ourselves and yet something other and greater than ourselves. Of the two parental figures, the mother is the less convincing for this purpose, because the mother is the parent we must break from in order to get born. To come into life is to be delivered from a mother, but the deliverance is temporary, and the emphasis on the male in the Bible is connected with its resistance to the cyclical fatality of all religions founded on Mother Nature.

The Genesis account of the fall speaks of two trees, the tree of life and the tree of forbidden knowledge. The latter clearly has something to do with the beginning of sexual experience as we know it, and is symbolized by a limp serpent crawling away on the ground. Metaphorically, the two trees would be the same tree, which would imply a tree of life with a fully erect serpent of wisdom climbing up its branches, as in the version of Indian yoga known as Kundalini. The sexuality of the tree of life would in that case have something about it of what has been called the myth of the lost phallus, a power of sexual experience where the relation of male to female has got free from the sado-masochistic cycle that dominates so much of our attitude to sex.

In the sexual creation myth with its earth-mother, the earth-mother is in the early stages of symbol of *natura naturans*, nature as a bursting forth of life and energy, its divine personalities the animating spirits of trees, mountains, rivers, and stones. This is the basis of what is called paganism, the instinctive faith of the *paganus* or peasant who is closest to the natural environment and furthest from the centre of the insulating envelope of culture. In the later stages of such 'paganism,' the preoccupation with cyclical movement climbs up into the sky and annexes the sense of *natura naturata*, nature as a structure or system which also manifests itself in cycles. Here the earth-mother expands into what Robert Graves calls the 'Triple Will,' the *diva triformis* or goddess of heaven, earth and hell, Luna, Diana, and Hecate, who meets us in so many other female trinities, the Fates, the Norns, the three goddesses confronting Paris. The cosmological vision such a myth suggests is one of cyclical fatality, where, as in the riddle of Oedipus, the three phases of infancy, manhood, and old age succeed one another without change.

At this point it becomes clear that the myth of creation is a part of a larger mythological structure known as the social contract. In paganism the contract which binds together the gods, mankind, and nature in a common recognition of law appears, for instance, at the end of Aeschylus' *Oresteia*, where the gods ratify the order of nature and to some extent are bound by it themselves. As paganism develops, it becomes clear by imperial Roman times that, as the gods grew out of nature-spirits, they are really expendable in this contract, the only essential god being the divine Caesar. In the biblical creation myth nature is not directly a party to the social contract, which is a 'testament' between God and man, nature having no law of its own except what God bestows on it. Thus in New Testament times the two creation myths had expanded into two contract myths focussed, one on Christ, whose divinity is an incarnation of God in man, the other on Caesar, who is Antichrist so far as he becomes a god by incarnating the link between moral and natural law.

As the longer and slower cycles complete themselves, there may be a sense of hope and renewal before the beginning of another cycle. At the time of Christ, when astrologers saw the sun moving into Pisces, many people talked about the dawn of a new and greater age, just as there are those who talk about an 'age of Aquarius' now. The most famous expression of this was Virgil's *Fourth Eclogue*, which predicts the arrival of a new golden or Saturnian age when 'the serpent shall die.' But although Christianity promptly seized on this poem as an unconscious prophecy of the birth of the Messiah, Christian writers also totally rejected all cyclical theories of history, whether hopeful or cynical in mood.

There are certain cultural disadvantages in an artificial creation myth, especially when presented as a deductive account of how the world and human life began. As what Plato in the *Timaeus* calls a probable narrative, or, as one translator has it, 'a likely story,' it reduces us to a passive role, inheriting the results of ancestral mistakes but unable to do anything about them. Thus the seventeenth-century New England poet Michael Wigglesworth represents the heathen at the Last Judgement objecting that it is hardly fair to send them to hell for Adam's sin, considering that they have never heard of Adam. They are told that Adam was designed to be a 'common root' of mankind, so that Adam's sin is their sin too, and they are compelled to agree, according to the poet, that the argument is irrefutable.

Then again, the conception of an artificer God, who starts everything off by making all things in more or less their present form, is not very encouraging for the human artist. If it is true that, as Sir Thomas Browne said, 'Nature is the Art of God'; if the models of human creation, the city and the garden, were created by God before man existed, the human artist seems to be in a hopeless position of competing with God. This is particularly true of painters and sculptors, who have often been regarded with suspicion as potentially makers of idols, dead images set up in rivalry with the maker of living ones. In Islamic culture this prejudice has gone to the point of banning representational art altogether, and similar tendencies have appeared in both Jewish and Christian traditions. In an early Christian romance called the 'Clementine Recognitions,' where the apostle Peter is the hero, some frescoes on a public building are referred to, and it is noted with approval that Peter is impervious to their artistic merit. There is no need to dwell on the iconoclastic movements that have swept over both East and West portions of the Christian world. As remarked in the first chapter, human creativity and divine creation often seem to be at loggerheads.

When painting and sculpture were tolerated, the religious prejudice against them carried on in some forms of critical theory, according to which artists in these areas were merely second-hand copyists of nature. Thus the Elizabethan critic George Puttenham, writing just before Shakespeare's time, says: 'In another respect we say art is neither an aider nor a surmounter but only a bare imitator of nature's works, following and counterfeiting her actions and effects, as the marmoset doth many countenances and gestures of man; of which sort are the arts of painting and carving.' Painting and sculpture flourished because artists and their patrons had the sense to ignore this kind of criticism; but there are other hazards in the conception of a prefabricated created order.

One of these hazards derived from the slow but steady advance of science. Whatever man creates is essentially a machine, an extension of his personality but with no life or will or its own. The effect of physical science, from Copernicus to Newton, was gradually to depersonalize the cosmos, as the earth was displaced from the centre of the universe and the angels from the guardianship of the planets. By the eighteenth century there was a general tendency to think even of the divine creation in terms of an ingenious and complicated mechanism. At the end of the century a standard textbook on natural theology, Paley's *Evidences of Christianity*, used the analogy of a primitive man picking up a watch on a seashore left by some passing mariner. The primitive was supposed to infer that a watch meant a watchmaker, and similarly we should infer that if a complex world exists, somebody must have designed the complications. Samuel Butler pointed out that this assumed primitive would be much more likely to make a god of the watch, as the Lilliputians thought Gulliver did with his watch when he told them that he seldom did anything without consulting it. But the analogy was regarded as a valid, even an unanswerable argument for a long time, and doubtless still is in some quarters.

The absurdities of the argument from design, more particularly of its illustrations, such as congratulating the Creator for his ingenuity in dividing the orange into sections for convenience in eating, had brought it into discredit even before Darwin's time. One cannot get very far with speculation on the mental level of a small child who assumes that a cat's tail is a specially designed handle for pulling it around. Yet the Darwinian revolution, transferring the designing power from God to a natural process, and showing that the argument from design was a projecting on God of the fact that man designs things, came as a profound shock to many intelligent people. Clearly the artificial myth of a creation had intellectual resources that we have so far not given it credit for.

The account of creation in Genesis is close to a group of sardonic folk tales, some of them much older than the Bible, that tell us how man had immortality nearly in his grasp, but was cheated out of it by malicious or frightened deities. It is hard to hear in its rather casual cadences what St Paul heard in it, the iron clang of a gate shut forever on human hopes. Neither is it easy to see in it the doctrine that man by his fall opened up a second and lower level of nature. The notion that nature fell with man is necessary to account for all imperfections in nature, ranging from human sin to thorns on the rosebush – an early Canadian Methodist circuit rider speaks of the clouds of mosquitoes he encountered in the New Brunswick forests as 'mementoes of the fall.' But the fall of nature has to be read into the Genesis account, because it is not there: we are told only that God cursed the ground, a curse he removed after the flood.

In many creation myths the creation starts off with an event that comes much closer than Sophocles' *Oedipus Rex* does to illustrating what Freud means by an Oedipus complex. A sky-father and an earth-mother are locked in connubial sleep until their son separates them, and creates an intervening world of air and light. Similarly in Genesis, light and air (the 'firmament') are created first: the firmament separates the waters above from the waters below, and according to the Book of Enoch the waters above are male and the waters below female. In Christianity it is also a Son who does the creating, though no female principle is involved at this stage. The Son, however, is identified with the Word that calls things into being: the Word says *fiat lux*, and

44

light appears. According to Hegel, creation is the symbol of absolute thought passing over into nature, nature being both the contrary and the dialectical complement of thought. Being a philosopher, Hegel assumed that the biblical Word and the philosopher's thought were essentially the same thing: poets, however, might see in the conception of a creating Word a more versatile power, capable of more things than dialectic. We seem to catch a glimpse, in fact, of a divine consciousness descending into experience. When man falls to a lower level of nature, the divine consciousness follows him there, until the process is completed by the Incarnation, the Word then becoming flesh, identical with human consciousness so far as it is human.

The assumption seems to be here that the term 'Word,' however metaphorical, has a very real connection with what in ordinary speech we mean by words, the elements of articulate consciousness. There are not many creation myths which give 'Word' so central a creative function: one of those that do is the Mayan Central American myth preserved in what is called the Popol Vuh. Here a primordial silence is broken by 'the word' which begins the story of creation: of all creatures, man is placed in authority because he alone could use articulate language, in contrast to the grunts and squeals of the beasts. But as man continued to praise his gods, the gods grew restive, and began to wonder if all this articulateness did not threaten their privileged position. Hence, as in many Near Eastern myths, the gods plot to destroy man by a deluge for fear he will become too big for his breeches.

Naturally the Genesis account cannot explicitly present God as jealous or frightened of man, but there is a curious suggestion of it:

And the Lord God said, Behold, the man is become as one of us, to know good and evil: and now, lest he put forth his hand, and take also of the tree of life, and eat, and live for ever: Therefore the Lord God sent him forth from the garden of Eden, to till the ground from whence he was taken.

Here God seems to be speaking to a council of other gods or angels, expressing a fear of some threat coming from mankind so great that he cannot even finish his sentence. It seems clear that man is in possession of something formidable connected with knowledge, whatever the knowledge of good and evil may imply. Even the Christian version of the myth implies that as soon as God speaks and becomes the Word of God, he has condemned himself to death; as soon as man falls with the power of speech, he becomes the potential murderer of God.

As further rationalized by Christian theology, this situation is explained as follows. Man is born into physical nature, the world of animals and plants, at least as they live at present, and this world is theologically 'fallen.' It was not the home originally destined for man, and man cannot adjust to it as the animals do. There is a higher order of nature which God intended man to live in, and everything that is good for man, such as law, morality, and religion, helps to raise him towards his own proper level of human nature. Many things are natural to man that are not natural to animals, such as consciousness, wearing clothes, being in a state of social discipline, and the like. In fact on this higher level of human nature there is really no distinction between nature and art. The complement of Sir Thomas Browne's principle that nature is the art of God is the principle that Edmund Burke was still insisting on at the end of the eighteenth century, that 'art is the nature of man.'

The agencies moving man upwards from his 'fallen' state to something closer to his original one certainly include law, religion, morality, and everything genuinely educational. Milton even defines education as the process of repairing the fall of Adam by regaining the true knowledge of God. Whether the arts belong among those educational agencies or not was much disputed. But a large body of opinion did see in this situation a function for the arts, more particularly the verbal arts. In Sidney's *Defence of Poetry*, for example, published around the time of Shakespeare's earlier plays, we are told that nature, meaning the lower or fallen physical order, presents us with a brazen world and the poets with a golden one; also that art develops a 'second nature,' being natural to man but only to him. Sidney's principle means that art, specifically poetry, can be tolerated in society only so long as, and so far as, its function is essentially an idealizing one. The arts form a rhetorical echo or chorus to the principles of morality and religion. They are there to persuade the more primitive and emotional side of man of the truth of what religion and morality teach, using concrete examples as a simpler analogy to the abstract precepts which are addressed to more mature minds.

Man, therefore, in the traditional Christian myth, is also born with a goal ahead of him, the raising of his state to the human level which is closer to what God intended for him. What is important about this for our present argument is that this means moving closer to the original vision of creation, so that creation here appears as the end of the human journey rather than the beginning of it. The central image of this in our literature is Dante's *Purgatorio*, where Dante adopts one of the oldest and most widespread symbolic images in the world, the spiral ascent up a mountain or tower to heaven, and makes it the journey of Dante himself as he climbs the mountain of purgatory, shedding one of the seven original sins at each spiral turn. The garden of Eden is at the summit: that is, Dante is moving backwards in time to his own original state, as he would have been if there had been no fall of Adam.

What we have now is a vision of two opposing movements, related to each other in what Yeats would call a double gyre. One is that of a divine consciousness being surrounded by experience as it descends from creation to the final identity of incarnation. The other is that of a human consciousness surrounding experience, as it ascends from its 'fallen' state towards what it was once designed to be. The ascending spiralling movement in Dante reminds us of Donne's image in his Third Satire:

> On a huge hill,
> Cragged, and steep, Truth stands, and he that will
> Reach her, about must, and about must go;
> And what the hill's suddenness resists, win so.

This human vision of recreation is heavily stressed in modern poetry, as in Yeats's 'Sailing to Byzantium,' where the sacred city is a human structure of art and yet preserves a vision of 'sages standing in God's holy fire.' Here creation has finally become one with recreation, and the revelation at the end of human effort is also a recognition of something at the beginning.

In the previous chapter I spoke of the association of human creative powers with two visions: the vision of the tradition of art in the past, and the vision of an idealized society projected on the future. Both these visions, I suggested, arise from a partial release of repression, a qualified escape from the encumbrances of ordinary experience. Beyond the *Purgatorio* vision in Dante lies the vision of the *Paradiso*. In the last canto of the *Paradiso*, after casually mentioning the story of the Sibyl who wrote her oracles on scattered leaves, Dante suddenly sees, in the very presence of God, the whole universe 'legato con amore in un volume,' bound into a single Word with love. As soon as Dante has this vision, it sinks to the lowest depths of repression: he forgot more of it, he says, than man has forgotten of his history since the Argonaut voyage. The implication is that immediately following the last vision of paradise, time moves back again to the opening of the *Inferno*, with the poet lost again in a tangled wood, where all the voices of repression, or what Dante calls *letargo*, 'lethargy,' start clamoring that there can never be any way out. But we are expected to see a bit more and forget less, and in particular to see that at the summit of the human journey back to the creation Dante's great poem merges into the vision of a God who is Alpha and Omega, the beginning and end of all verbal possibilities.

Dante's journey is a journey back to the creation, the journey of a creature returning to his creator, and the initiative for the journey does not come from Dante himself. It is the energy and grace of the descending movement of the divine word, working through such intermediaries as Beatrice, which impel Dante and make what he does possible. Even in the revolutionary Milton, writing over three centuries later than Dante, man still has no real initiative: liberty, for example, in Milton is nothing that man naturally wants, but is something God is determined he shall have. But within another century or so we begin to move into the intellectual climate we still live in now. Here the central characteristic of traditional myth, the model or plan that existed before the beginning of time which repeats itself constantly in present human life, has totally disappeared. The majority of poets and thinkers today see no model or plan, no human essence or general human nature, established at the beginning of things, only various mutations imposed by cultural and social change. In the next chapter I should like to look at this situation and at some of its results and effects.

3

I N THE FIRST TWO CHAPTERS I have tried to suggest that there are two ways of approaching the notion of creation. There is a traditional myth of creation in which God brings the world into being before man, who is himself a later part of creation. The models of human civilization are supplied by God, who plants a garden and places Adam in it, and who created an angelic city before there were any human cities. This creation was, we are told, perfect, or at least 'very good,' whatever the source of this value-judgement. Man lost touch with the divine creation through his own sin and 'fall,' and now lives in an alienating nature in consequence. The other approach to creation starts with the vision that man has of a nature recreated in humanized form, the vision recorded in various forms of the arts, ranging from pastoral poetry to architecture. It culminates in a vision of recreation in which man himself participates, and which appears to be in fact the total aim and goal of human creative effort.

I discussed in the second chapter some of the impoverishing qualities of the myth of a special divine creation. In its more rigid form, at least, it assumes that the arts are only feeble and pointless imitations of what God has done infinitely better; it goes into bewildering verbal quibbles in efforts to 'reconcile' God's goodness and the world's badness, and it becomes increasingly isolated from everything that the sciences have to tell us about human origins. The myth itself has a built-in explanation for its own sterility. It contains the implication that our minds have been too clouded over by the fall to respond directly to a vision of divine creation, and can only learn something about it on a level that we can fit into our existing mental categories. Thus W.H. Auden makes his Simeon say, in his 'Christmas Oratorio' *For the Time Being*, that man's consciousness extends only to the limit of what is traditionally called original sin, of which 'it is impossible for him to become conscious because it is itself what conditions his will to knowledge.' So, accepting the myth on its own terms, we can never get back to the vision of creation before the fall in our imaginations, however carefully we study the Genesis account. The myth speaks of an angel who guards the tree of life, whose flaming sword symbolizes the blinded mental conditions in which we approach it.

In the previous chapter I tried to show how in Dante the vision of the future goal of human recreation takes the form essentially of a return to God, a return which is also a response to God's initial effort to descend to man. The close of the *Paradiso* is the summing up of centuries of thought in which a view of creation derived from the Bible provided a conception of two levels of nature, an upper level which is man's original home, and is identical with the state of art, and a lower level which is the physical nature of plants and animals, and is not man's home but only his environment.

Everything that raises man from his fallen level to his originally designed one involves some degree of returning to his original creation. It is recreation only in the sense that man is included in it: the actual process is God's redemption of man, man doing very little for himself that is of any real use. The whole process of human response, in Christian doctrine, is contained within the Holy Spirit, so that man's redemption is a drama within the persons of the Trinity in which man has a very limited actor's role. As the Holy Spirit guides the church, the doctrine of the Trinity, which is so central to Christian dogma in both Catholic and Protestant contexts, seems to have been, in its historical setting, a doctrine designed primarily to prevent man from slipping out of the grip of the church.

This view is part of an authoritarian structure, and a great deal of its power and influence collapsed under the hammering of the great capitalist revolutions of the eighteenth century. In the nineteenth century we see that the mythological picture which survived Dante for many centuries has finally and totally changed. There is no longer any functional place for a divine creation myth at the beginning of things: there is only human culture, and therefore at most only the sense of human recreation as a distant goal. But human culture and its goals are not guaranteed by anything like a universe of law rooted in the nature of God himself, much less by any will on the part of a God to redeem. On the contrary, they are guaranteed by nothing and are threatened by practically everything. Everywhere we turn in the nineteenth century, we find a construct reminding us of a Noah's ark bearing the whole surviving life of a world struggling to keep afloat in a universal storm. We have Schopenhauer's world of idea threatened by a world of will, Marx's ascendant-class culture

threatened by a dispossessed proletariat, Freud's ego cling-
ing to its precarious structure of sanity and threatened by
the forces of the libido, Nietzsche's morality threatened by
the will to power, Huxley's ethical values threatened by the
evolutionary drive. These various thinkers take various attitudes of sympathy or hostility towards the threatening force,
but the mythical construct is of much the same shape in
every one.

Heidegger says that the first question of philosophy is
'why are there things rather than nothing?', but surely there
is an even prior question: why objectify the world at all? or,
more simply, why do we want to know? It sounds like a
psychological question, but it is only partly that. The
moment we ask it we are involved in the whole process of
what I have called recreation, the constructing of human culture and civilization, and the question turns into something
more like: 'why is simple existence in the world not good
enough for us?' Whatever the answer, the question itself
seems to push us away from the biblical story of a beginning
creation, and towards the vision of recreation as a future
goal in which our own efforts are involved.

This lands us in the antithesis of the traditional Christian
view, a secular attitude in which man as at present consti-
tuted has to be regarded as himself the only creator in question. The end of human recreation, then, finds humanity
looking at itself in a mirror. This is a somewhat daunting
prospect: Narcissus at least had a beautiful face to look at,
but the face of humanity that would look out of such a mirror is that of a psychotic ape. I discussed in the first chapter
the fact that paranoia is a part of the secular attitude, and the
two poles of paranoia are quite obviously present here, as
they are in all the Noah's ark constructs just mentioned. If

we select certain facts and attend only to them, we are the lords of creation and recreation alike, with an infinite destiny before us: if we select others, we summon up a vision of hideous and total eclipse in a hydrogen bomb Armageddon. The gospels represent Jesus as continually casting devils out of the mentally ill: we may regard this as primitive psychology, and feel that is is unreasonable to expect modern man, living in this advanced century of Hitler and Idi Amin and Mr Jones of Guyana, to believe in evil spirits. But in other moods we may recognize that the mentally ill who know that they are possessed by devils are in a sense the lucky ones, and that the rest of us are similarly possessed but don't mind. The older construct wore out because it repressed the sense of human autonomy, the awareness that there are more things in man than any church or government can recognize or accommodate. But a purely secular construct, whether humanist or Communist, may be repressing complementary things.

The first person in the modern world who understood that the older mythological construct had collapsed was William Blake. He also, though without direct influence, set up the model for all the nineteenth century constructs just mentioned, where cultural values float on a perilous sea. In Blake we begin with the *Songs of Innocence*, which reflect a child's view of the world, in which the world is controlled by a benevolent providence, makes human sense and responds to the human need for love and peace, and was probably made in the first place for the child's own special benefit. As the child grows older, he enters the world of 'experience,' and learns as an adult that the world is not in the least like this. At that point his personality splits in two. His conscious waking adult self, which Blake calls Urizen, struggles to adapt itself to what for it is the real world; his childhood vision, which Blake calls Orc, is driven underground into what we call the subconscious, where it forms a boiling volcanic world of mainly sexual and largely frustrated desire.

A typical song of innocence is the poem called 'The Lamb,' where a child asks a lamb the first question of the catechism, 'Who made thee?' He knows the answer: Jesus made both the lamb and the child himself, and Jesus is also a lamb and a child, a creator whose creation is 'very good' because it is identifiable with his nature. The counterpart to 'The Lamb' in the *Songs of Experience* is 'The Tyger.' Here, instead of one question promptly and confidently answered, we have a long series of rhetorical questions without any answers, culminating in the crucial question, 'Did he who made the lamb make thee?' This question also has no answer, because in the world of the tiger, the world our adult minds inhabit, the conception of a divine creator makes no sense. The tiger, as Blake sees him, is one of the forms of the angel guarding the tree of life, or what Blake calls the Covering Cherub. Perhaps we can eventually get past him to some vision of creation which will include his glowing and sinister splendour. But such a vision of creation would have to be at the end of a long journey to somewhere on the far side of the tiger. There can be no going back to square one and the child's vision of the lamb. This long-range vision of creation would also have to include and incorporate our own creative powers: we cannot go back either to a ready-made order supplied us by a pre-existing providence.

But Blake, though he destroys a mythology derived from the Bible, is an intensely biblical poet himself. He reads the Bible in what he calls its infernal or diabolical sense. According to him the creation of the world, the fall of man, and the deluge of Noah were all the same event, and the fall was a fall in the divine as well as the human nature. Hence what has traditionally been called the creation is actually a ruin, and there is no creation except human recreation, which is the same humanized form of nature that we find in the paradisal, pastoral, agricultural, and urban imagery of the Bible. Blake is far more interested than the Bible itself is, however, in seeing the relevance of the human arts to this transformation of nature. He speaks of poetry, painting, and music as the three forms of conversing with paradise which the flood did not sweep away.

Blake's perspective on the theme of creation in the Bible begins with the Book of Exodus, with Israel in Egypt and a situation of injustice and exploitation already present. God intervenes in this situation, telling Moses from the burning bush that he is about to give himself a name and a highly partisan role in history, taking the side of the oppressed proletariat and holding out to them the goal of a 'Promised Land' of their own, which they will have to work towards. Man has to depend at least partly on his own imagination and creative powers to lead him towards the goal symbolized in the Bible by its last book, the Book of Revelation, Blake's favourite biblical book, where the form of the world that man should be living in is set out at the very end, following visions of appalling disasters before that end is reached. The vision of a created order is never an easily attained vision, but comes out of the depths of human anguish and effort. One very clear example in the Bible is the 'Song of the Three Children' in the Apocrypha, meaning the three Jews in Babylon who were flung into Nebuchadnezzar's fiery furnace because they would not abjure their faith. It was from the midst of the fire that they sang their hymn of praise to God for his beautiful world, just as the hymns of praise in the Psalms and elsewhere come out of Israel's deliverance from the 'furnace of iron' which is what Egypt is called by Solomon.

In Blake's illustrations to the Book of Job, made towards the end of his life, the same attitude to the structure and imagery of the Bible is equally clear. What the Book of Job seems to be saying, as we follow its argument through the deadlocks caused first by Job's three friends and then by Elihu, is that God himself intervenes in the discussion to convict Job of ignorance. He asks Job a series of rhetorical questions about whether he was present at the original creation or could do any of the things then done. Job wasn't and couldn't, and God seems to regard this as a triumphant argument in favour of the wisdom of his ways and the folly of Job's. For Blake, however, God is not indulging in crass bullying: he is telling Job that how he got in his situation is less important than how he is to get out of it again. Job is being pushed away from the creation and all efforts to find his way back to a first cause, and encouraged to look in the opposite direction, where he can see the alienating forms of nature, symbolized by the behemoth and leviathan who appear at the end, as the sources of the repressions, internal and external, which are preventing him from seeing his own original birthright.

Blake's reading of the Bible is so deeply rooted in the structure and imagery of the Bible that it is perhaps worth asking what principle his reading is based on. We cannot read far in the Bible, of course, without becoming aware of the importance of all the standard figures of speech, of which the most important is metaphor. In metaphor, we have two points of verbal reference existing together: 'this is that.' But there are also at least two figures of speech that exist in time. The more familiar of these is causality, which may be suggested by some things that go on in nature, but as a way of arranging words is a rhetorical figure of speech. The verbal progression in causal writing is normally forward from cause to effect: this becomes that, or, this results from that. But the mental operations preceding the writing out of the causal sequence move backwards. The causal thinker is confronted by a mass of phenomena which he can understand only by thinking of them as effects, after which he searches for their preceding causes. The movement backwards reminds us of, and may even be connected with, Plato's conception of knowledge as recollection. Present things are understood by being related to past things in such a way that cognition becomes the same thing as re-cognition, awareness that a present effect is a past cause in another form. Causality is, of course, an essential basis of both scientific and metaphysical thinking, and its verbal expression is that of continuous prose, which seems to have been developed mainly for the purpose of putting causality into verbal structures.

The Bible is based mainly on another figure of speech which also moves in time, but in the opposite direction from causality. This is the figure traditionally called typology. In the Christian view of the Bible, everything that happens in the Old Testament is a 'type' or 'figure' of which the New Testament provides the 'antitype' or revealed meaning. Thus Paul (Romans 5:14) speaks of Adam as a *typos* of Christ, and I Peter 3:21 speaks of Christian baptism as the *antitypos* of the story of the flood. Such typology is not confined to the Christian perspective: the Old Testament, from a Jewish point of view, is quite as typological without the New Testament as with it, and its antitypes are still the restoration of Israel and the coming of the Messiah, though the context of these events is different from that of Christianity.

Typology is clearly not, like causality, anything that can be linked to a scientific or philosophical procedure. It belongs in the area indicated by such words as faith, hope, and vision. It has some affinities with allegory: the stories or myths of the Old Testament become types or parables of existential truths, and many parts of the Old Testament, such as the ceremonial law, have usually been read allegorically by Christians. But the normal structure of allegory, an imaginary narrative paralleled with the moral precepts which are its 'real meaning,' does not fit the Bible, where both Testaments are concerned with actual people and events. What typology really is is a vision of history, or more accurately of historical process. It insists that for all the chaos and waste in human effort, nevertheless historical events, or some of them, are going somewhere and meaning something. Our modern belief in historical process, whether it takes a democratic or a Marxist form, is an outgrowth of the cultural legacy of the Bible.

In the nineteenth century the conception of evolution suggested certain analogies in human life that gave us a new form of typological thinking. This was because evolution was interpreted purely from the human point of view. Evolution, as we see it, did the best it possibly could when it finally produced us, and whatever more it can do it can do only through us. Hence the kind of typology symbolized by science fiction and by all the forecasts of the future based on present technology: everything we can do now is a type of what we shall be able to do in the future. I spoke a moment ago of the manic-depressive insanity of these and similar attitudes as they shuttle wildly from dreams of unqualified progress to nightmares of unqualified disaster.

Kierkegaard wrote a small book on *Repetition* in which he proposed to adopt this term as a characteristic of Christian philosophy, one which is thrown forward to the future and is at once a contrast and a complement to the Platonic view of knowledge as recollection of the past. The Christian repetition, Kierkegaard says, finds its final formulation in the apocalyptic promise 'Behold, I make all things new.' It seems to me that Kierkegaard's idea is derived from, as it is certainly connected with, the typological structure of the Bible. In any case the typology of the Bible links it to history in a way impossible for paganism, which remains based on the recurring cycles of nature. To use fairly familiar terms in a slightly different context, biblical mythology is diachronic, pagan mythology synchronic. The diachronic dimension makes it possible for personality to emerge in biblical mythology. Jesus and Adonis are both dying gods, with very similar cults and imagery attached to them, but Jesus is a person and Adonis is not, however many human figures may have represented him. Nietzsche drew from evolution a diachronic vision of human self-transcendence which he called the Superman. But his preference for the synchronic Dionysus over the diachronic Christ forced him to enclose his Superman in a framework of identical recurrence which for me, and I should imagine for others too, totally destroys the dynamic of the conception.

At the same time typology cannot preserve its vitality indefinitely unless it keeps its antitypes in the future. By making the Old Testament a historical process fulfilled in the coming of Christ, Christianity was in danger of losing this

vitality as that event receded into the past. A 'second coming' or future transcendence of history had to grow up along
with the doctrine of the Incarnation, and is very prominent
in every part of the New Testament itself, but had to lead an
increasingly furtive existence as the authority of the Church
grew and history, like the Marxist state, continued to fail to
wither away. What happened, in practice if not in theory,
was that the entire Bible, including the New Testament,
became a type or parable of which the antitype or revealed
form was the structure of Christian doctrine as taught by the
church. The role of the doctrine of the Trinity in this process
has already been considered.

Some of the Protestant Reformers attempted to cut away
this superstructure of doctrine in favour of a more direct
dialogue with the Bible. The degree of their success does not
concern us here, except for one major work of literature
involved with it, Milton's *Paradise Lost*. We have suggested
that an artificial creation myth, with its implication that
everything man can do has already been done by God on an
infinitely superior plane of reality, is a somewhat hampering
one for the human creative impulse. Why, then, did the
instinct of so very great a poet lead him in precisely the
direction of retelling the story of creation in Genesis, and to
retell it expressly for the purpose of rationalizing it, or, as he
says, to justify the ways of God to men? It is an attempt to
answer this question that takes up the rest of what I have to
say, although the answer will take us a long way from Milton.

The basis of Milton's thinking is Paul's conception of the
gospel as the fulfilment, or what we are calling the antitype,
the revealed form, of the Old Testament law. The external
acts prescribed for the specific nation of Israel become what
Milton calls 'shadowy types' of an individual's inner state of

mind. Again, the law is the myth, the type, the parable; the gospel is the existential reality that the law symbolizes. Similarly, the story of creation functions as a type or model of that inner state of mind in which Adam, at the end of the poem, begins the long climb up towards his original home again. Eden as an external environment disappears, to reappear as the 'paradise within thee, happier far,' which is held out to Adam as a final hope. Once more, the creation myth is a seed that comes to its own real fruition in a recreative effort in which Adam is involved. Adam is, of course, the representative human being, or, more precisely, the representative reader of the Bible. The Bible is in effect being read to him through the last two books of the poem.

It may sound fatuous to say that *Paradise Lost* was written for the sake of its readers, but Milton's more discerning critics have always recognized that there is something very distinctive about the role of the reader in that poem. Many critics have asked who the hero of *Paradise Lost* is, and have given various answers: Satan, Adam, Christ. But there is a lurking feeling that the question is somehow inappropriate. In Milton's theology the supreme authority is not the Bible but the reader of the Bible, the person who understands it and possesses what Milton calls the word of God in the heart. From one point of view we can say that this is not the reader as human being, but the Holy Spirit within the reader, so that Milton is keeping the whole operation wrapped up inside God, as his orthodox contemporaries did. But there is enough vagueness and indecision in Milton's view of the Holy Spirit to make it clear that he is moving in the modern direction of regarding the reader, simply as human being, as the real focus of his poem and the final aim of all his 'justifying' of the ways of God.

In my first chapter I quoted a passage from Oscar Wilde's essay 'The Critic as Artist.' This essay builds up an argument that seems to make an exaggerated and quite unrealistic importance out of the reader of literature, the critic being the representative reader. He is paralleled with the artist in a way that seems to give him an equal share at least in what the artist is doing. Here again Wilde is writing from the point of view of a later generation. For many centuries the centre of gravity in literature was the hero, the man whose deeds the poet celebrated. As society slowly changed its shape, the hero modulated to the 'character,' and in Wilde's day it was still the creation of character, as one sees it so impressively in Shakespeare, Dickens, and Browning, that was the primary mark of poetic power. At the same time the Romantic movement had brought with it a shift of interest from the hero to the poet himself, as not merely the creator of the hero but as the person whose inner life was the real, as distinct from the projected, subject of the poem. There resulted an extraordinary mystique of creativity, in which the artist became somehow a unique if not actually superior species of human being, with qualities of prophet, genius, wise man, and social leader. Wilde realized that in a short time the centre of gravity in literature and critical theory would shift again, this time from the poet to the reader. The dividing line in English literature is probably *Finnegans Wake*, where it is so obvious that the reader has a heroic role to play.

The literary critic of 1980 finds himself in the midst of a bewildering array of problems which seem to focus mainly on the reader of a text. What is a text, and what does a reader do to it when he reads it? Where is the text – in the book, in the reader's mind, or lost somewhere between? If a work of literature is read and appreciated centuries later than it was written, what is the social context of its meaning? Some of these questions may be peripheral, or resolved only by some kind of dead-end paradox, but the issue they relate to is still a central one. It seems to me that, once again, some such conception as that of 'recreation' is needed to make sense of such problems. Every reader recreates what he reads: even if he is reading a letter from a personal friend he is still recreating it into his own personal orbit. Recreation of this sort always involves some kind of translation. To read is invariably to translate to some degree, however well one knows the language of what is read.

Let us take translation in its customary sense of changing a structure from one language to another, as a special case of recreation. The question of translation is peculiarly important in the Christian tradition, which has had a close connection with translation from the beginning. Moslem and Jewish scholarship are, inevitably, bound up with the linguistic features of the Arabic of the Koran and the Hebrew of the Old Testament respectively. But the New Testament was written in a *koine* Greek unlikely to have been the native language of its authors; and when those authors used the Old Testament, whatever their knowledge of Hebrew, they normally relied on the Septuagint Greek version. Then for over a thousand years the only Bible available in Western Europe was a Latin Bible, and modern movements from Luther to the missionary work of the nineteenth century brought with them a strong impulse to translate the Bible into every known tongue.

Everyone concerned with the study of literature knows how much of translation is a settling for the second best. This is most obvious in major poetry, where a translation has to be a miracle of tact without claiming to be a replacement for the original. The particular problem we are concerned with, however, is of a different kind. The cynical Italian proverb *traditore traduttore*, a translator is a traitor, has two points of reference. Granted sufficient scholarship, a translator does not necessarily betray his text: what he always does and must betray is his own cultural orbit, the socially conditioned limits within which he can operate. The English reader looking for translations of Homer can find an exuberant Elizabethan Homer in Chapman, a periwigged Homer in Pope, a Gothic-revival Homer in the Loeb Classics, a colloquial modern Homer in the Penguins. What he will never get in this world is simply Homer in English.

Similarly with the Bible. There may be something of Paul in the 1611 translation: 'Charity suffereth long, and is kind; charity envieth not; charity vaunteth not itself, is not puffed up.' But we also hear the anxieties of 1611, when the clouds of civil war were gathering and the British Empire was getting started with settlements in America and the founding of the East India Company, and where ambition and aggression seemed the most dangerous foes of charity. In fact Shakespeare's Wolsey, denouncing ambition at roughly the same time, employs a very similar figure to 'is not puffed up' when he speaks of himself as having ventured beyond his depth like little boys swimming on bladders. There may be something of Paul too in the modern Phillips translation: 'This love of which I speak is slow to lose patience – it looks for a way of being constructive. It is not possessive: it is neither anxious to impress nor does it cherish inflated ideas of its own importance.' But there are also the anxieties of middle-class democracy in these cadences, of a world where charity has a good deal to do with being a co-operative committee man.

At this point, translation merges into the wider question of recreation. What can be translated is what is loosely called sense, the relation of many signifiers to a common signified. Each reader, translator or recreator, renders his text into a form determined largely by his own cultural context. To return to the terms of our first lecture, the arts form an extension of our own past, but find their meaning for us in our present situation. That present situation contains elements of vision which we project on the future, and those elements form the recreating aspect of our reading. Every work of literature that we continue to read and study meant something to its own time and something quite different to us. Both poles of understanding have to be kept in mind. If we disregard its original historical context, we are simply kidnapping it into the orbit of our own concerns; if we disregard its relevance to ourselves, we are leaving it unrevived in the morgue of the past. But if we keep the two together and in balance, we are stabilizing a tradition, and are engaged in a process which includes ourselves and yet is something bigger than ourselves. One end of this process is a creation, and the other end a recreation.

There is another aspect of recreation, however, which expands into the whole history of language itself as a form of human communication and consciousness. We mentioned Homer, who is one of the purest poets we have, because his language comes from a time before abstract or conceptual thinking had developed. Homer's vocabulary, as Onians' monumental study of it, *Origins of European Thought*, shows us at length, is astonishingly concrete. Such conceptions as anger, cunning, thought, emotion, are all solidly anchored in parts of the physical body, such as the diaphragm and lungs. This means essentially that Homer's vocabulary was not metaphorical to him, but must be to us. The metaphor is the figure of speech that expresses most clearly the sense of an identity between subjective and objective worlds, and Homer comes from a time when no very clear line was drawn between them. Since then, there have been several other developments in language, one of them the descriptive language of our own day, which is based on a clear separation between subject and object, between element of personality and element of nature. It is one of the functions of literature in our day, more particularly of poetry, to keep reviving the metaphorical habit of mind, the primitive sense of identity between subject and object which is most clearly expressed in the pagan 'god,' who is at once a personality and a natural image.

This means that the cultural affinities of poetry are with the primitive and archaic, a fact about poetry which has been recognized from early times. The metaphors of poetry take us back to a world of undifferentiated energy and continuous presence. Take these lines from a well-known hymn:

> His chariots of wrath the deep thunderclouds form,
> And dark is his path on the wings of the storm.

We may not be deeply moved by these lines – I am not presenting them as major poetry – but we could be by other lines as far removed from descriptive or objective meaning as they are. If we took them 'literally,' whatever that means, we should have an intolerably crude notion of the God they attempt to describe. But, of course, we do not take them in that way; we take them as poetic metaphor. Like other hymns, this one draws on the Bible, and in one of the Psalms it is said that God rode upon the back of a cherub, and did fly. But there the statement is still poetic metaphor. Some mythical rationalizers might want to carry the image back to a society so confused about nature that they would 'believe' that thunder indicated a God riding around the sky in some sort of private aeroplane. But it is not necessary to assume that any such society ever existed: the statement is *radically* metaphorical. It is a way, perhaps the only type of way, that language has of conveying the sense of a numinous presence in nature, and that is where we stop. We notice incidentally that in these lines the Christian God is being represented by *a* god. In spite of the achievement of Dante and Milton, poets on the whole feel easier with pagan gods than with the Christian God, because pagan gods are ready-made metaphors, and go into poetry with the minimum of adjustment.

We think of the creation story in Genesis as essentially a poetic account. For Milton it was not a poetic account, yet he deliberately poeticizes it. By doing so he turned it into an intricate body of metaphors, conveying the sense of a spiritual force that includes man but does not originate from him. It is particularly in the account of creation itself, in Book Seven, that we realize how the poetic paraphrase renders our sense of creation, not in an ornamental or sophisticated form, but in a far more primitive form than the original does:

> Forth flourished thick the clust'ring vine, forth crept
> The smelling gourd, up stood the corny reed
> Embattled in her field: add the humble shrub,
> And bush with frizzled hair implicit: last
> Rose, as in dance, the stately trees.

The recreation of poetry and its metaphorical use of language leads to two principles, one specific, the other universal. First, it reveals the narrowness of our ordinary descriptive use of language. Nietzsche's statement 'God is dead,' which has been so widely accepted, even in theological circles, is primarily a linguistic statement, or, more precisely, a statement about the limitations of language. The word God is a noun, which within our present descriptive framework of language means that God has to belong to the category of things and objects. We may agree that God is dead as the subject or object of a human predicate. But perhaps using the word God as a noun in this way is merely a fallacy of the type that Whitehead calls misplaced concreteness. We note that in the burning bush story in Exodus, God, though he also gives himself a name, defines himself as 'I am that I am,' which scholars say would be better rendered as 'I will be what I will be.' Buckminster Fuller wrote a book called *I Seem to be a Verb*, and perhaps God is a verb too, not simply a verb of asserted existence but a verb expressing a process fulfilling itself. Such a use of language revives an archaic mode of language, and yet is oddly contemporary with, for example, the language of the nuclear physicists, who no longer think of their atoms and electrons as things but as something more like traces of processes.

Then again, the traditional doctrine of divine creation, we said, is creation with what we ordinarily mean by words. We have tried to show how the recreating of language attaches man to words in such a way that words become something much bigger than he is, hence we can well understand such thinkers as Heidegger and others when they suggest that language is not a machine or invention that man uses, but something that, in its full range, uses man, man being ultimately the servant rather than the master of language. There is a further suggestion that there may be something linked to the human use of words which is a power of human self-transcendence, a step away from the narrow humanism that has to stop with the psychotic ape in the mirror.

There is also the term 'spirit,' which is so emphasized in the New Testament, with its insistence that the scriptures have to be 'spiritually discerned.' One of the things that 'spiritually' must mean in this context is 'metaphorically.' Thus the Book of Revelation speaks of a 'great city, which spiritually is called Sodom and Egypt' and is also identified with the earthly Jerusalem. And one wonders, in studying Hegel's *Phenomenology of the Spirit*, which has become a text used by Christians and Marxists alike, whether the antithesis of theist and atheist in our day may not be a quarrel of Tweedledee and Tweedledum over a word that neither really understands. For the atheist is still left with personality as the highest category in his cosmos after he has rejected the *theos*.

The terms 'Word' and 'Spirit,' then, may be understood in their traditional context as divine persons able and willing to redeem mankind. They may be also understood as qualities of self-transcendence within man himself, capable of pulling him out of the psychosis that every news bulletin brings us so much evidence for. I am suggesting that these two modes of understanding are not contradictory or mutually exclusive, but dialectically identical. Certainly the goal of human recreation, whenever we try to visualize it, bears a curious resemblance to the traditional vision of divine creation at the source. As the fully awakened beings in Blake's *Four Zoas* say: 'How is it that all things are chang'd, even as in ancient time?'

To extend the meanings of 'word' and 'spirit' into areas beyond the human seems to make them into objects of belief.

But it seems to me that there are two levels of belief. There is, first, professed belief, what we say we believe, think we believe, believe we believe. Professed belief is essentially a statement of loyalty or adherence to a specific community: what we say we believe defines us as Christians or Moslems or Marxists or whatever. But then there is another level in which our belief is what our actions show that we believe. With some highly integrated people the two levels are consistent. But professed belief, in our world, is pluralistic and competitive. It is characteristic of believing communities, anxious for their solidarity, to set up elaborate structures of faith that ask too much from their adherents in the way of professed belief, forgetting that any belief which cannot become an axiom of behaviour is not merely useless but dangerous. In some respects professed belief is a solid and satisfying basis for a community, yet in our world it seems that it is the worst possible basis for a *secular* community. Whether the community is nominally Catholic or Protestant or Jewish or Moslem or Hindu, every secular state guided by religious principles seems to turn them into a form of devil-worship. The same thing is true of Marxism, which when it becomes socially established acquires a religious quality based on the doctrine of the infallibility of the Holy Communist Church. In the Soviet Union, as more recently in China, periodic 'thaws,' or pretences at democratic tolerance, take place for the purpose of discovering who the really dangerous people are, ie, the people who do not subscribe to this doctrine of infallibility.

If there is a creative force in the world which is greater than the purely human one, we shall not find it on the level of professed belief, but only on a level of common action and social vision. At this level all beliefs become to some degree partial, not because they are untrue for those who hold them, but because the human mind is finite and the human will corrupt. To work within such a community no one needs to surrender or even compromise with a professed belief. But those whose professed belief is Christian, for example, would be recognizing the supremacy of charity over faith which is part of that faith itself, as well as the gospel's insistence on 'fruits' as the only valid proof of belief. This conception is close to what Blake, in a phrase taken from the Book of Revelation, calls the 'everlasting gospel,' a conception which implies that the human race already knows what it ought to be thinking and doing, though the voices of repression, made articulate by competing ideologies, keep shouting the knowledge down. They are all voices of Antichrist, whose first act recorded in the Bible was to build the Tower of Babel to the accompaniment of a confusion of tongues.

Every unit is a whole to which various parts are subordinate, and every unit is in turn a part of a larger whole. Religions, theistic or atheistic, are units which define themselves in such a way as to cut off the possibility of their being parts of larger wholes, even when they are compelled to act in that way by expediency. We are perhaps now in a period of history at which this looks more like pride and delusion than like faith. If we could transcend the level of professed belief, and reach the level of a world-wide community of action and charity, we should discover a new creative power in man altogether. Except that it would not be new, but the power of the genuine Word and Spirit, the power that has created all our works of culture and imagination, and is still ready to recreate both our society and ourselves.

Notes

References sufficiently identified in the text are not given here.

p 5, line 24. 'Wordsworth.' 'The Tables Turned' 16

p 6, line 1. 'Vico.' *The New Science of Giambattista Vico*, tr. Bergin and Fisch (1968), section 331

line 30. 'Heidegger.' *An Introduction to Metaphysics*, tr. Manheim (1959)

p 7, line 17 'Frazer.' Apollodorus, *The Library* (Loeb tr., 1921) xxvii

p 11, line 12. 'Decreation.' Cf. Wallace Stevens, *The Necessary Angel* (1951) 174

p 12, line 8. 'Emily Dickinson.' *Letters* (Belknap Press 1958) II, 576

p 14, line 6. 'Joyce's phrase.' *Ulysses* (Random House ed. 1934) 35

p 15, line 18. 'Jacques Lacan.' *The Language of the Self*, tr. Wilden (1968) 18

p 19, line 24. 'Marcel Duchamp.' *The Green Box*, tr. Hamilton (1957)

p 25, line 2. 'Eliot.' 'Burnt Norton' 65

p 28, line 26. 'Samuel Butler.' *Life and Habit*, Ch. 7

p 32, line 21. 'Milton.' *Paradise Lost*, I, 741
p 34, line 10. 'St Augustine.' *Confessions*, Bk 12
p 37, line 25. 'Aristotle.' *Metaphysics*, section 988a
p 39, line 7. 'Robert Graves.' 'To Juan at the Winter Solstice' 9
p 40, line 21. 'Michael Wigglesworth.' *The Day of Doom*, sts
172-81
line 31. 'Sir Thomas Browne.' *Religio Medici*, The First Part
p 41, line 22. 'Puttenham.' *Elizabethan Critical Essays*, ed. Gregory
Smith, II, 188
p 43, line 14. 'circuit-rider.' *Literary History of Canada*, ed. Klinck
(1965) 130 (actually Lower Canada)
line 28. 'Book of Enoch.' I Enoch, section 54
p 44, line 1. 'Hegel.' *Phenomenology of the Spirit*, section 774
line 20. 'Popol Vuh.' *Popol Vuh, The Sacred Book of the
Ancient Quiche Maya*, 1950, 82ff
p 45, line 31. 'Edmund Burke.' *Appeal from New to Old Whigs*
p 46, line 11. 'Sidney.' *Elizabethan Critical Essays*, ed. Gregory
Smith, I, 156
p 48, line 8. 'Dante.' *Paradiso* xxxiii
p 58, line 5. 'Solomon.' I Kings 8:51
p 59, line 25. 'typology.' See Auerbach, *Scenes from the Drama of
European Literature* (1973). The essay on 'Figura,' 11-76, is
practically indispensable.
p 66, line 22. 'Shakespeare's Wolsey.' *Henry VIII*, III, ii, 359
p 68, line 28. 'one of the Psalms.' Psalm 18:10 (cf. II Samuel
22:11)
p 70, line 28. 'Heidegger.' *Poetry, Language, Thought*, tr. Hofstadter
(1971) 198
p 83, line 10. 'everlasting gospel.' Revelation 14:6